Joie de

PAUL BA⸱⸱⸱⸱

CB *editions*

First published in 2022
by CB editions
146 Percy Road London W12 9QL
www.cbeditions.com

Printed in England by Blissetts, Brentford, TW8 9EX

ISBN 978–1–909585–45–4

For David Perry and Tim Dee
inquisitive spirits

It was one of those bleak days when you just wonder what you're on earth for in the first place and why you're going to so much trouble to stay here.

– Georges Simenon, *Maigret at Picratt's*,
translated by William Hobson

I have passed all my days in London . . . the innumerable trades, tradesmen, coaches, wagons, playhouses, all the bustle and wickedness round about Covent Garden, the very women of the Town, the Watchmen, drunken scenes, rattles – life awake, if you awake, at all hours of the night. I often shed tears in the motley Strand from fullness of joy at so much Life.

– Charles Lamb in a letter to William Wordsworth,
declining an offer to visit Cumberland, 1801

ACKNOWLEDGEMENTS

Some of these poems first appeared in the *New Statesman*, the *Guardian* ('Poem of the Week') and *Salmagundi* (US).

My special thanks are due to Georgina Hammick, Michèle Roberts, Lindesay Irvine, Benedict Warren and Sandro Melani.

Contents

For J.

Our love's defined by laughter now.
The sound of it warms us.
It fills the house on our happiest days.
You'd never guess, if you chanced upon us,
that once we had sorrowing grief in common.

November 28, 2020

Joie de vivre

I have a battery that keeps me ticking.
I think I take at least twenty pills a day.
I laugh when I can and weep when I must.
I love and am loved. Oh, it ought to become a psalm,
this catalogue I'm setting down
with measured sorrow and delight
in the very first hour of an April morning.

It's All Fools' Day right now.
I listen to my waste making its way
into the stoma that I've had to wear
for ten confusing months
and almost marvel at the sound it's making.

My body's not what it was.
It's been opened up and put back together
too many discomforting times.
It seems a stranger to me when I need to look at it.

There are hyacinths and tulips in the garden
and a few distraught daffodils
and the untrustworthy camellia's about to blossom.

April 1, 2020

3

Dawning

I awoke this morning curled like a foetus.

It was as if I'd been encased again –
dependent upon my mother's breath
on some invisible winter's day
before I was hauled out into a world
of startling light
I was hesitant to enter

but which now, many seasons later,
I am reluctant to leave.

The Wanderer

At first, I thought he was setting off for work each morning, but as the years went by I came to realise that the man who was customarily dressed in black and never without a cigarette had no job to go to. He was walking with a purpose to nowhere in particular.

It continues to be his destination, although his stride remains purposeful. There's determination in his features as he marches forward, stabbing at his mouth with the cigarette he has recently lit from the glow of its predecessor. On he goes, up and down the streets of the neighbourhood, before returning to the house five doors from mine where he rents a flat or a furnished room, perhaps.

I have often wondered where and how he acquires his money, because smoking to excess is a costly habit. It could be that he was left a substantial sum by a parent or relative which he has invested wisely and that his stark manner of living belies his wealth. I have met shabbily dressed rich people, but none of them seemed as self-contained as he is. It's as if the world around him is a mere backdrop to his overriding concern of walking with fortitude in a series of circles.

Or so I imagined, or persuaded myself to believe, until last July, when I saw him in what, for me, was a surprising situation. The strange individual I had been observing for over a decade from the vantage of my writing table by the window had stopped in the street and was talking to someone. I was returning from the dentist, I remember, and had not anticipated what was happening. I began to walk at a slower pace as I approached the man with the perpetual cigarette and the chic young woman, whose work involves meetings with gentlemen callers during the course of the day, and discovered that they were speaking Polish, he with conspicuous animation. She was holding her pampered toy dog to her generous bosom and was laughing loudly at something he'd said. He was laughing, too, between puffs, and his eyes, usually so indifferent to the passing scene, were glittering. I was startled, I admit, by this sudden, spontaneous display of happiness. I was tempted for a second to greet them in their language and add something inconsequential about the lovely weather, but caution prevailed and I walked on, their laughter continuing behind me.

It's October now, and the steadfast walker is as he always was before that hot summer afternoon. He looks like Raskolnikov again. The constant rain of the past few days hasn't deterred him. He has a hooded black jacket and even an umbrella. There's no hint of subdued or forthcoming laughter in his haggard face. He is himself once more, or so I care to imagine – the solitary mystic with the absurd ambition to walk onwards and ever onwards towards something on the horizon only he can see.

Perseverance.

Dunmore would be a friend.

Snapshot

For Georgina Hammick

Someone has taken a photograph of them
on a Sunday afternoon, I imagine,
in a London park.

She's wearing a cloche hat.
He's in his shirtsleeves, looking almost happy,
sitting beside her on the summer grass.

Who took the picture?
A friend, or an obliging stranger,
nearly a century ago?

The woman's my mother and the almost-happy man,
smiling rather against his will,
is her husband-to-be.

She would learn, in their twenty years of marriage,
that almost-happiness
was the best they could ever bargain for.

Wartime

There were six sardines in the tin
and five of us at the kitchen table.
Mother mashed up the fishes with margarine
and portioned them out on toast.

This was our special treat –
the last we enjoyed in the house
that would be rubble in the morning.

Rejuvenation

I never dreamed that I'd grow old.
An early death was on the cards
or in the stars, for me.

There are days now when I wish
I'd given up the ghost
or met my Maker –
whoever that is –
with someone weeping at my bedside
long years ago.

But, what the fuck, I'm here –
sustained by medicine and metal –
and writing the poetry
I knew I'd write, but didn't,
before I evaporated
at the age of thirty,
or thirty-one at the latest
at a gasping pinch.

Ah, the dulcet clichés
of the Romantic imagination.

Death's a vivid acquaintance.
He, she or they is creeping up on me.

I think that I've become a master of evasion.

Homecoming

There was an orange waiting for me
when I came home from the special hospital
at the age of five.

My father peeled it for me.
My mother broke it into segments,
carefully, one at a time,

and fed the little boy
she called her mistake.

I couldn't eat all of it,
so she took a piece and he took a piece,
and my brother and sister
each had a piece

and we were, perhaps,
the happiest of happy families.

Afterwards

The fog has lifted.
The sky's its usual grey
except for the whiteness of a crescent moon
above the gasworks.

It's a London November
and I am looking at the moon
as if it's an approachable friend.
A year has passed since my father died.
I'm twelve and already prone to melancholy.

Ages and ages later
with a confused and confusing life behind me
I see the moon again.
It's distant now and unapproachable
as it always really was,
as it always has to be.

Strange how the sudden sighting
of a crescent moon
shining faintly above the gasworks
once gave me comfort.

Lovely for the thought.

Bouquet

I bought my mum a bunch of flowers once.
The florist picked them and arranged them for me.
He said I was a very thoughtful son
as he took the note I offered him
and pressed the change into my hand.

My mother shoved the roses and veronica
and the fine white spray
into a vase
and told me that my tea was ready.

I watched the flowers wilt and die.
I was to become increasingly observant.

Spring Flowers

When I asked my mother where her father was
she told me he was pushing up the daisies.

My father's father was doing just the same
though he'd started earlier in life,
before he even reached the age of thirty,
she sighed.

I think I guessed what she meant
in her riddle-prone way
as she garlanded death
for the five-year-old son
who'd been restored to her.

Legacies

Dandelions and daisies
and lobelias gone wild
blossomed every spring
on London's bomb sites.

There were other flowers, too,
with fanciful, poetic names
I stopped and picked
and then arranged in jam jars.

I thought, when I was ten,
that they were gifts from the dead
who lay beneath the ragged grass
still undiscovered.

Speechless

My mother let out a howl
like some demented animal
on a December morning
while she waited for the butcher
to trim a shin of beef
for our Sunday dinner.

Her husband was newly dead
and recently buried
when the anguish of his going
made her abandon words –
her mainstay; her sarcastic safety net –
the better to yelp
at being trapped or caged
in something unavoidable.

And then she pulled herself together,
and then she said she didn't know
whatever had come over her
and then she smiled as she paid the butcher
and ruffled my hair
and ushered me out of the shop.

And that, for ever afterwards, was that.

Trojan

My mother was christened Helen Maud
during one of the last Victorian Septembers,
but when she gave birth to me –
dangerously late in life –
she was no longer Helen.

The people who said that she worked like a Trojan
didn't have Helen of Troy in mind.
The woman they praised was the reliable Maud –
a deeply respectful mother and wife
and the best of all possible servants.
She was the salt of the earth, if anyone was.
They wished there were more of her kind in the world.

There were more than enough of her kind in the world I
      grew up in:
Maud's sisters, Maud's friends, those hosts of similar Mauds
who worked their 'fingers to the bone',
as they were proud of stating.
My childhood was engulfed by them.

After Maud's death, I had a glimpse of Helen
in a photo taken sometime in the 1920s.
Helen's eyes are shining, while her smiling lips
seem to be poised for seduction.
She could be Clara Bow or Theda Bara, a temptress of the
      silver screen,
ready to spread herself out on an ottoman
covered in tiger skin.
The man behind the camera must be fancying her rotten
as she gives him the come-on.

My mother a vamp? I thought of the legendary Helen
launching those fated thousand ships
and heard Maud's voice berating me.

I was to know my place, Maud said.
I was to marry and settle down
and be a respectable breadwinner.

Maud reminded her son, in excess of the thousandth time,
that the trouble with having brains is that they give you ideas.

Good Lad.

Charity

For My Nieces

My mother's darning my dead father's socks
and I'm wondering why.

There's one particular pair she smiles upon.
I'm wondering again.

She finds a different needle and a stronger thread
to make them look the way they looked
when he first wore them.

So I suppose as she works away
until it's time to draw the curtains
and boil the milk for cocoa.

'Some poor soul's feet will be happier with these,'
I hear her say
as she closes her knitting basket
and removes what she calls her 'special' glasses.

Provision

My mother started saving for her funeral
the year her husband died.
He'd had a respectable sending-off
in a big black car with a mountain of flowers on top
and friends in attendance.

There was even a grave to prove that he had lived.

She needed all those things.
She'd grown up with a fear of destitution.
What more could she want
than a few nice words at the end
and a hymn or two
and the knowledge in the congregation
that she'd never left a bill unpaid?

Dead Letter

To my mother

I'm closer to you now –
I need to tell you –
than I ever was in life.

You have become my comforting,
not my unsettling, shade.
You're bringing me grieving happiness.

It has to be your ghostly gift to me –
this never-anticipated radiance,
this state of something very close to love
between us.

The Staff of Life

I open the curtains and see there's a rain-soaked bread roll on the pavement opposite our house. As I'm looking, the ginger-and-white stray cat turns the corner and stops to examine it. He lifts it up with his paws, gives it a sniff, decides not to eat it and plays with it instead. He taps it into the gutter and sets off again on his daily hunt for real food. When he's safely out of sight, a pigeon dives down from the rowan tree and starts pecking at it. The bird is interrupted by a boy on a skateboard and flies off. The roll is in the middle of the road now. A magpie swoops down from a roof nearby and while it's attempting to eat the roll, I'm thinking of the old woman in a village in Transylvania who advised me to count backwards from thirteen to zero in order to ward off any harm the sighting of a solitary magpie might bring. Just as I am doing as she told me, an approaching car scares the scavenger into flight. The astute creature returns to the roll and is joined, seconds later, by a crow. They begin cawing and croaking at one another, but their squabble is brought to an end by a woman on a motor-bike honking the horn. Soon there are cars coming and going in both directions and the bread roll, miraculously, somehow remains unsquashed. A drunk, who occasionally waves to me as he passes, suddenly appears. He's already swaying, although it's only 8.15 in the morning. Crossing the road, he is drawn to a halt by the bread roll, which he stares at. He bends down and picks it up. Like the cat before him, he sniffs it. He brushes it with the sleeve of his well-worn jacket. He takes a tentative bite. He waits. Then he nods and smiles approvingly. He gives a thumbs-up to himself and decides to eat. He is happily munching on it as he walks unsteadily away.

Pilgrimage

For the Rivar Goddesses

I'm old and my hair is white
and my health's unsteady
and I have too many grievances
against the uncaring world.

I want one thing. It isn't much to ask.
I share with Petrarch the desire
to go back to Rome –
not to hanker after a lost love
as he was prone to
nor to display obeisance to the God
that Michelangelo
almost made manifest.

No. I've a simpler need.
It's to return again to a little restaurant
where the waiters are elderly,
even older than I am now,
and surly in that peculiar Roman manner
I came to marvel at.
I had to learn their caustic language
before they smiled on me.

Serenity

For Sandro Melani

The restaurant on via Santo Spirito
always offered *zuppa di fagioli*
on Thursdays.

I would order a large bowl of it
as well as a flask of Chianti
and eat and drink

and wonder at the simple happiness
of eating Florentine beans
and drinking rich red wine
and being alive.

It was my custom afterwards
if the weather was fine
to walk uphill to the Piazzale Michelangelo

propelled all the way by the starch
in my contented stomach.
I farted and paused for breath and farted again

until I reached the Forte Belvedere
where I stopped and marvelled
at the pink and green and gold
of the paradisal city
spread out below.

Raised by Hand

I was a gloom before I was a gay.
I imagined, or believed, that I was fated
to die some kind of martyr's death
because of my desires.

That's how it was. That's how it used to be.

The cinema offered consolation.
I gave myself to Marlon Brando
hundreds of crazily wonder-struck times
in my small back bedroom
overlooking the railway,
bending – you might say – to his will,
especially when his muscle-bound torso
was dripping wet.

There was always gloominess afterwards
when guilt informed my stiffening handkerchief
that I'd been bad, and worse than bad,
to let my less-than-natural feelings
take such possession of me.

Seventy years have passed.
Now I am gloomily gay, or gaily gloomy,
and philosophical.

Tar Brush

The pimples on his chest
were the only flaws on his body
that I could see.

There were nine in total.
I checked the number
each time I looked at him
in the changing room.

He was the only dark boy in the school.
The words 'tar brush' were whispered about him.
'A touch of the tar brush' meant
that he had one white parent and one black.
I didn't care which.

He cupped his hand on my arse once.
I turned and wondered at his smiling face,
then sent him a prudish scowl.
I wish I hadn't. For years and years and years
I wished I hadn't.

Reflective

It's the summer of 1955
and I'm in a bedsit in Vauxhall
with the Jamaican I love so hard inside me
I ought to be screaming
but somehow I'm not. Somehow
I'm thinking of my dad, who's dead,
and my mum, who's waiting at home for me,
being shocked and horrified
at the thought of their brave little boy
surrendering himself
in such a shameful way
at a time of night
when respectable people
should be safely asleep.

Bestowal

You had it made for me
while you were turbulently dying,
the delicate gold necklace
I've worn for thirty-five years.

It's all I have of you and want of you.
It's always been enough.

'This is for you,' I heard that evening
as you pressed the little box into my hand
and warned me that I didn't have to like it.

Were those your abstruse words of love?
I've cared, and care, to think so.

It's when I'm parted from that fragile gift
in hospitals – for scans and ECGs and X-rays
and complicated operations –
that I most keenly feel the loss of you.

You had it made for me.
You paid the goldsmith who designed it.
You had it made with me in mind.

Parting

after Anonimo, circa 1250–1300

Leave, my love, farewell.
You have stayed here too long.
The morning bells have sounded.
I fear the day will soon reveal us.

Leave, my love. Let us say goodbye
before some evil, jealous one discovers
this hideaway I've found.
Be quick, and dress yourself.
Kiss me, my sweet.
You are my heart's enchantment.
We're lovers now, true lovers,
and will remain together,
I promise you.

Leave, leave, my love. Farewell, goodbye.
Go quickly, quickly.
No one can ever part us, once we're safe.
But now, just now, my dearest only love,
go away quickly, quickly . . .

Sparrowhawk

after Anonimo, circa 1250–1300

For Miranda Richardson

I am lost without the sparrowhawk
I have loved for years.
He was obedient to my every call
but now he has gone from me.
I am still sick with love for him
because he has flown –
higher than he ever flew before –
into another woman's garden.

I fed you, my sparrowhawk,
I cared for you.
I gave you a golden bell to wear,
such was your beauty.
In dreams I hear you boasting
that you've risen up like the sea
and broken the chains that bound you.

There were no chains, my sparrowhawk.
I see you on your perch,
flapping your wings,
and hoping, hoping
they will guide you back to me,
my sparrowhawk.

T. H. White.

Dora's Dinner Party

On that warm May evening, Dora served the two of us a memorable meal in the kitchen of her studio flat. It began with a Greek lemon soup, the recipe for which she had cajoled out of the chef at a very special taverna in Crete. Yes, she had *cajoled* it out of him, she repeated, savouring her new English word.

Dora was German, but not happily so. The subject of Germany was not to be mentioned in her company. It was strictly *verboten*. She had told us very little about her past, and what she had told us, she insisted, was more than enough. The little we knew was that she had been born and raised in Cologne, where she met her future husband, an English film director who was making a documentary about the school from which she had recently graduated. That was in 1947. A year later, they were married and living in London, in the mews house near the Thames she still occupied. They were together for just over five years. Then he committed suicide. He had received an income tax demand for £3,500, which he was unable to pay. He had taken the coward's way out. And that was that. *Kaput*.

Dora had never talked about this man in loving terms. She was in her late teens when they began seeing each other and he was nearing thirty. She had found him clever, like the best kind of teacher. He was widely read, as the books in his possession testified. It was his mind and his wit that mattered to her and the fact that he was taking her away – for ever, she hoped – from a country she had begun to loathe.

The table was made ready for the main course – a roast leg of lamb with sprigs of rosemary and baby onions – she had already removed from the gas oven, the door of which she left slightly ajar. While the meat was *settling*, she pointed at the oven and informed us, in an almost jocular fashion, that it was there that he did it. I heard myself asking, stupidly: Which he? Did what?

She looked at me and said I was slow off the mark tonight. He was her husband, late husband, Gavin, and what he did, for which she would never forgive him, never while she lived and breathed, was to stick his head in the oven, with the unlit gas full on, and breathe in the fumes until he was dead. That's what he did. Right there.

She closed the door of the oven. The meat was now rested. It had *settled*.

The image of Gavin lying on the kitchen floor, with his head in the oven, inhaling the lethal fumes, stayed with me as I enjoyed the taste of the lamb, the onions, the spring greens, the gravy and the freshly made sauce with the mint from Dora's 'window-box herb garden'.

The apple tart that followed had been baked in the same oven earlier in the day, I realised.

We played two games of Monopoly that night. Dora was excessively delighted to win both of them.

My companion and I made 'Gavin's oven' part of our private language. We still used it, very occasionally, in the years after Dora had replaced it with a brand-new electric model.

In Winter

There was nowhere else to go, it seemed,
in Venice, in that dank December,
when the waiter suggested that we make *amore*
as he handed me the bill.

I was staying at the Hotel Fenice
which was charging out-of-season prices
for its sumptuous bedrooms,
so I didn't understand when he insisted
that the *albergo* was *troppo raffinato*
for our kind of love-making.
He might be recognised
and laughed at and mocked
for being a *finocchio*.
He could lose his job.
He pulled a sad face as he spoke.

Giacomo had to catch the last train back to Mestre
where he lived with his parents.
We had an hour at most.
He knew a graveyard in a nearby *calle*
behind a church where no one worshipped.

Oh, the sweet madness of it.
He led me to a mildewed tomb
on which we sat and kissed
and unzipped and unbuckled
and frantically gratified our mutual lust.
Una tempesta, he said, after we'd come together.

We hugged when we parted, in the Italian manner.

There was a recital at the Teatro Fenice that night,
I sat on a step by the stage door
and listened to Brendel playing
Schubert's last piano sonata
before I entered the hotel
in a strangely contented mood
and went to the bar
and ordered a glass of champagne
with which I silently thanked Giacomo
for our death-denying adventure.

Situation poems.
or which prioritise
a narrative
event

When events become
a story, poetry is
mastered —
fe the dimensional
quality needed.

Transport

The Styx ought to be everywhere you look.
I speak from experience.
I went for a trip on it once,
without my knowing.

I fell for the ferryman,
who seemed to take a shine to me
with his glittering black eyes
which promised adventure.

I lost weight within days
of that first hypnotic encounter.
It wasn't a miracle cure,
that rapid shedding of flesh,
that sudden opportunity to voyage
into unknown places
I'd scarcely dreamt of:

Istanbul, Izmir and Antalya
were all on our lustful agenda.

He wasn't called Charon, of course.
It's not a name you'd foist upon your child
in Turkey, or elsewhere, or anywhere,
when you stop to think about it.

Only parents of a morbid disposition,
possessed of a sinister sense of humour,
would bless, or curse, their son
with such a tell-tale moniker.

But Charon he was, I remember,
and the boat he navigated
often hit turbulent waters.
He had another passenger
who left him millions.

The Styx ought to be everywhere one looks –
not out of sight and out of mind
as it was for me.

Employment

Charlene wakes Matt at four a.m.,
while their twins are still asleep.
He has a working week ahead of him.
He's going to be Spence Clench for five long days.

'It's Spence time, honey,' she reminds him,
in case he's forgotten, which he hasn't.
'Jeez, babe,' he mumbles. 'I better douche again.'
He's wanted at the studios at six.

Matt's butt's his cash cow – no denying.
Spence Clench has made him famous
to millions of perves who cream themselves
watching him being porked.

He's twenty-seven now and almost past his peak.
His face and ass require make-up.
It's difficult staying boyish.

Charlene looks lovingly at him. He studies his schedule.
'I gotta coupla scenes with Jackson Shooter,
but Wednesday's the problem.'

Wednesday, he's well aware, means double penetration.
This week he'll have two cokeheads dicking him.
They'll take forever getting boners
for the irresistible Spence Clench.
Buster Delcazzo will need some pussy pics
to make him halfway hard enough.

'Ciao, Matt. Hi, Spence,' says Charlene
to her crazy, but crazy, husband.
'Have fun,' she adds. 'Have lots of it.'

Matt thinks of Jake and Jolene
once he's in the limo.
They owe their future to his butt.

The sun comes up. It promises to be
another beautiful day in San Diego.

Show Business

For Roberta Taylor and Peter Guinness

The recently blinded Duke of Gloucester
has both his vile jellies back in place
as he stands in the glare of the footlights
taking his bow.
He's a blinking miracle.

Regan and Goneril, arm in arm,
curtsey in unison.
They blow fond kisses to the audience.
They're models of kindness
as they turn and beam at one another.

Edgar and Edmund seem to be reunited
in fraternal affection.
It's Edmund who ruffles his half-brother's hair
before he kisses him.
You'd almost think they're lovers.
They are.

Kent strides on to the stage and nods,
and nods again, and goes on nodding
as he retreats into the wings.

The Fool seems disconcerted
by the warmth of his reception.
He stays incredulous, in character.

The younger-looking Lear, his wig askew,
is staggering beneath the weight
of his daughter Cordelia

whom he holds aloft in his middle-aged arms.
He's glad that it's the last performance
and that he'll never, never, never, never, never
have to act with the stuck-up little cunt again.

The cast take their final calls
then gather together, hand-in-hand,
bowing and bowing and bowing
until the heavy safety curtain
lands with a thud at their feet.

lovely

Philosophical

The young American introduced himself as Darius Laclotte.

That's an arresting name, I said.

You think so? The second bit's French.

I thanked him for the explanation and asked if his ancestors had been settlers from France.

It's of no importance to me. I have other things to consider.

Of course you do. Shall we discuss your work?

Why not?

You sent me three pages. Of a short story? Of a novel? You haven't made it clear.

Fiction. Whatever.

It's very difficult for me to say something constructive with so little to work on.

I appreciate that. He smiled, as if to accentuate his appreciation of the difficulties I faced. I really do.

Another page arrived by email. Then, after a few days, yet another appeared. The story, or whatever it was, was making no progress. The words were slowly mounting up, but the prose remained inert.

On his second visit to my house, he wore a leather jacket, leather trousers and shiny black leather boots. I wondered if he was trying to convey a sexual message, before dismissing the idea as risible. I refrained from saying that he was dressed rather strangely for such a warm summer's day.

We were discussing, in a fashion that can only be described as roundabout, the five pages I had set out on a table, when my elderly tortoise-and-white cat, who was called Puss, padded softly into the room. She edged towards the visitor who, catching sight of her, jumped to his feet and screamed.

She's old, I said. She's ancient. She's harmless.

He was panting as he told me hated cats. They terrified him. They were nasty. They carried a curse with them.

I picked up Puss, stroked her head, and carried her downstairs and let her out into the back garden.

He was still catching his breath when I returned to the sitting-room. I poured him a glass of iced lemonade and waited for him to calm down.

I'm actually a philosopher, he announced suddenly. I have no intention of becoming a creative writer like you. I want a master's degree, that's all.

Why aren't you studying philosophy?

I have no need to.

Are you serious, Darius?

Very, very serious. Never more serious.

Which philosophers have influenced you? Thoreau, perhaps? Emerson?

Nope.

David Hume? John Locke?

He shook his head.

Schopenhauer?

No. No one. It's my philosophy. I don't have influences. I have my own ideas. I influence myself.

You do?

Yup. That's what I'm telling you.

I felt inspired to ask if it was possible for me to read his – how could I put it? – philosophical writing?

No, he answered. That's a definite negative. No. Definitely not.

Why is that?

Because I haven't written it yet is why. It isn't ready. I will let you into a secret, though. My philosophy will be in one big single book.

Like the Bible?

Correct. Once I have written it, when it tells me it's ready, I will have it printed. Just one copy. Then I will buy a large tin box and

41

put it inside. I will lock the box and bury the key with the box in my folks' yard.

You will?

Yes. And I will leave instructions that it's not to be opened for a thousand years. By that time, my prophecies will be fulfilled.

Your prophecies?

Exactly so.

There were obvious questions arising from these pronouce-ments, but I was too bemused and exhausted to bother to ask them. It was early evening by now. I offered him a glass of wine or a refreshing beer.

I do not drink alcohol. It destroys the brain.

Yes, I suppose it does, I said.

He got up to leave. He wanted to use the bathroom before he went, but only if it was safe from the nasty cat.

She has her own resources, I assured him.

I gave a reading from my latest novel in a bookshop and after-wards I signed copies for several people who wished to buy it. And there, standing before me, was the smiling Darius Laclotte with the book open in his hands. I said how pleased I was to see him again and then inscribed my novel with his name and a friendly message and the date beneath it.

He frowned when he saw the inscription.

You've put Darius Laclotte in it. That's wrong. I'm not Darius Laclotte anymore.

I can change it for you, I said hastily. I can alter it.

No. I should have told you. I stopped being Darius Laclotte yesterday.

Who are you now?

Someone different.

He sent me twelve-and-a-half pages of his story or whatever before he disappeared. I kept them in the computer until it crashed some

42

years later. They went the same way as other, more important and indeed precious, documents that were lost irretrievably.

I can always say that I once knew a handsome American who called himself Darius Laclotte for reasons beyond my reckoning. He has left me his name to conjure with.

Paolo's Leap

We could be laughing tonight
as we always laughed together
whenever we met.

You once remarked that we were
connoisseurs of silliness.

I think I've hated you since 1979
when you abandoned all your mirth
and leapt from the fifth-floor balcony
of a mansion in Paris
onto the cobbles below.

'I must have been emulating Floria Tosca,'
I heard you whisper to me
as I was rinsing the wine glasses
after supper.

You weren't, of course,
but it was kind of you to say so
in the quizzically humorous voice
that was yours alone.

Nocturnal

I knew a man once who wished he hadn't been born.
He meant what he said.
He wasn't a poseur.
In the few, radiant years I knew him
He never spoke for effect.

He said what he meant, I remember,
quietly, thoughtfully,
over tea and scrambled eggs on toast
on one of those perfect mornings
that always follows
a night of rapture.

He had the bright way of speaking
of those in the deepest despair.
He made himself a joy to be with.
He saw the funny side of almost everything.

I knew he had meant what he said
when he departed decorously
with sleeping pills and vodka.
No noose, no razor blades, no blood in the bath,
and nothing so wickedly inconsiderate
as a sudden plunge under an oncoming train –
he valued understatement.

I shan't reveal his name.
He wouldn't have wanted me to.
He really did prefer oblivion.
It was his chosen habitat.

Goodness

For Rosalind Sippy

He spoke more to my dog than he did to me
on that September afternoon,
because his right leg suddenly excited her,
making him blush and laugh.
He called her a beauty and advised her to calm down
and stop behaving like a shameless hussy.
His eyes gleamed while he stroked her.

He'd come up from Wales to collect your ashes.
He said he didn't know what to say
when he took the urn from me.
He'd arranged with a priest in Abergavenny
to have your remains buried alongside the mother
who'd lauded you and denigrated him.

The dog was licking his face
when he remarked, without resentment,
that you and Mam would be happily reunited
for all eternity.

He knew – we all knew – that you'd died of drink.
I offered him a glass of something, nonetheless.
He took a long time answering.

'All things considered, what with him in mind,
and seeing that it's a special occasion,
I'll settle for a lager, if you have one.'

We sat in silence as we drank.
He stared at his watch.

'Time to be off. Time to get back to the family.'
He kissed the dog goodbye.
He shook my hand.
I paid my respects to his wife and children.

'I'll post you a photo of the gravestone'
were his last words to me.

Shopping

i.m. Vanni Bartolozzi, December 1946 – September 2001

That was to be your last outing,
and what a spree you had, buying
eighty-two pairs of Armani underpants
in a single afternoon.

Why eighty-two? That was your special secret,
along with the six suitcases, the ten
cashmere sweaters and the dozen overcoats –
each one identical.

Your joyful madness was halted in Amsterdam
by the brother whose profligacy in youth
had so distressed you. He was solvent now
and sensibly married, the comforter

who packed the underpants, the sweaters
and the overcoats into six suitcases
and drove you home to Florence, where
your long imprisonment began.

You lost all memory of that last outing.
You lost much else besides – your wit, your grace,
those reams of precious poetry you'd known by heart.
All gone. All vanished. Nothing was left

except a desolate awareness. Your bulbous,
frightened eyes spoke what you couldn't say.

The underpants became a family joke.
'*Ottanta-due,*' your mother said, and smiled.
'*Perché ottanta-due?*' She shook her head.
You'd left behind a comic mystery.

Gathering

For Keith Parker

I like their company most on sunlit days
when I see and hear them at their cheeriest.

That's when they're glad to be alive
and I am, too.

I sometimes share a drink with them
on late afternoons
with the light fading softly around us . . .

Then suddenly it's evening
and a second bottle of wine
appears on the table.

The time has come to be reflective,
to talk of the past, such as it is,
and the future, perhaps,
of which we're uncertain.

They flee from me at nightfall
and I'm alone again
and happier for it,
knowing that they'll return
in the clothes they used to wear.

Fabulous

As she was dying
the painter and storyteller
envisioned hosts of blackbirds
on the white walls of the room.

'They're singing for me now,' she told the son
sitting at her bedside,
ever-so-gently pressing
the hand he held in his.

When she turned to him and smiled,
he knew that the birds had flown
and the singing was done.

Performances

I last saw Jean a year before she died.
We had a bibulous lunch to celebrate her freedom –
champagne, red wine, and a single malt with her coffee.

'Oh, love, I'm so relieved,' she said.
'I may not look it, but I'm young again
with all my spots and wrinkles.'

She'd been a dominatrix for ten lost years,
playing an ever-so-easy-to-outrage Nanny
in a Bayswater basement flat

she'd bought from a friend called Karen,
an Austrian who looked like a Rhine maiden
and was a demon with her leather accessories.

'Talk about the Ride of the Valkyries,'
Jean chortled. 'She gave them a run for their money
as soon as she came out with *Achtung*

or *I hef vays of making you soffer,
Schweinhund.*' Dear Jesus, Karen was a laugh-
and-a-half, if ever she knew one.

'It got to her, dear, all that play-acting.
She was exhausted by it. She went back to Vienna
and pigged herself on *strüdel*

and now she's a great big happy balloon
with her girlfriend who likes them chubby.
Good luck to her, I say.'

Jean had to find a different kind of client.
She lacked the venomous energy
Karen had made her trademark.

'She taught me how to be a maiden lady,
a vicar's daughter would you bloody believe? –
who expected young boys to respect their elders

and never indulge in bad behaviour.'
Jean's own young boys, she told me,
were seldom younger than fifty

and most of them, her regulars,
were in their sixties, seventies and eighties.
Her naughtiest young boy had hired her services

on his hundredth birthday. After she'd smacked him hard –
and even harder, as his special treat –
he showed his Nanny the congratulatory letter

he'd received from her gracious Majesty the Queen,
    God bless her.
'Oh, his old bum was smarting, I can tell you. And the
    tears he shed
when Miss Enid Sharpley announced her retirement.'

'Those were the days,' Jean muttered.
She hadn't kissed or touched a single one of them.
There'd been no fondness, no embracing –

simply a script to act by rote,
a cane or strap or belt with which to inflict
the necessary, always-paid-for pain.

Most of her clients arrived by taxi.
They wore corduroy trousers in garish colours.
She often watched them on her television

at Prime Minister's Question Time
complaining that our once-proud British nation
was becoming a nanny state.

'They speak from experience, don't they?'
Jean smiled at me and I smiled back
at the kindly warrior who'd become my friend.

To Sadie

Dearest Sadie,

I can't expect you to remember the dictionary definition of *poudrette*. It's from the French, of course, and it dates from 1840. I am pleased to remind you, now, that it's a manure made of night-soil mixed with charcoal. Someone, somewhere, is probably finding a good use for it as I write.

But on that happy evening in the late 1970s, when the four of us played the definitions game after dinner, *poudrette* had a different meaning for you. A *poudrette*, you wrote on the slip of paper you passed on to the player with the correct meaning in hand, 'is a ladies' lavatory attendant in the Cameroons'.

Oh, Sadie, I'm still smiling. The idea that a *poudrette* is a woman paid to look after the needs of richer women in a high-class public toilet is strangely plausible. I can hear the clicking of beringed fingers as her special services are called for: *'Ici, poudrette, ici, tout de suite.'* It's the setting you chose, the Cameroons, that makes your interpretation of the word so funny.

You greeted me with the words 'I've put on my wig for you' the next, and last, time I saw you some months later in the hospice.

'I look less of a fright when I'm wearing it.'

I had brought you champagne at your request. You already had several bottles by your bedside and there were more in the fridge.

'Enough for a lifetime,' you joked.

We shared a half-bottle that sunlit afternoon.

'I can just about taste it,' I can remember you saying.

An old man shuffled into the room, apologised for interrupting us, and asked Sadie how she was doing.

'Never been better,' you replied, and he said, 'That's all right, then. I'll leave you in peace', and went away.

You told me that Jimmy was one of the residents. He wasn't

alone in treating the place like a luxury hotel. 'He really believes he'll be going home soon.'

We talked for another ten minutes or so before you said you felt wretchedly tired. It was time to take off the Mata Hari wig and lie down.

We kissed each other, continental fashion, and said goodbye.

You called out to me to take care of myself when I was halfway down the corridor.

I never got to tell you what happened next, Sadie. So anxious was I to be out in the sunshine again, in the tree-lined street, that I pressed the wrong button when I entered the lift. Instead of stopping at G, for the ground floor, it sped downwards to LB, the lower basement. The doors opened to reveal a children's playground. Cries of 'Hello, Mister' greeted me. The boys and girls stopped their game to smile and stare at a new visitor. A bald little boy, clutching a red ball, came towards me, inviting me to play. His happiness, like that of his playmates, filled me with terror, I have to confess to you. I found myself pressing and pressing the G button. 'Mister?' the boy wondered loudly as the doors closed on him.

I should have spoken to the child. I should have told him I wasn't allowed to play with him. I could have said I was sorry, at the very least.

There was much laughter, you will be pleased to hear, at the farewell party you paid for. Ex-lovers spoke of you fondly as they ate the canapes and drank Veuve Clicquot. After what someone observed as sounding like a religious ceremony – The Scattering of the Ashes – a three-course meal would be served.

Your daughter invited everyone into the small garden alongside the studio apartment to see her scatter your ashes under the gingko tree you nurtured over many years.

At the very moment the urn was opened, and its contents shaken in the direction of the gingko, a sudden gust of wind sent them flying into the faces of the surprised mourners. We were flicking all that was left of you off our clothes, shaking you out of our hair, picking tiny bits of you out of our bubbly.

'We seem to be drinking Sadie,' said the handsome television presenter who was the only famous guest there that day.

It was generally agreed that the gust of wind was your idea. You'd planned for it to happen. Everything, you were telling us, must end with laughter.

Oh, Sadie, I remember you saying to me once that you toiled in the Augean Stables of literature, finding willing ghosts to write the memoirs of the footballers, golfers, cricketers, tennis players you represented. And comedians, too – they were by far the most unpleasant and venal of your clients. You had witnessed life in the raw and had somehow survived. You enjoyed being described as 'blowsy', a Cleopatra transformed into Mistress Quickly. You revelled in the fact that the surname you inherited from your husband made you sound, appropriately, like a Woman with a Past.

Sadie, my mischievous friend for all too short a time, I picture you now as a champion of *poudrettes* everywhere, fighting for their cause to remind privileged ladies to clean up after themselves, *merci beaucoup*.

With my lasting love,

P.

Curriculum Vitae

after the poem in Kurdish by Sherko Bekas

For Azad Shawkat Beck

When the first people were fleeing, I fled.
When the first fires were started, I was burnt.
When water first covered the face of the earth, I drowned.
When the first knives were sharpened, I was cut to shreds.
When the first lands were apportioned, I was cast aside.
When the first trees were felled and chopped up to make timber
I was the first to be hanged on the very first gallows.

I was a refugee before Moses.
I was crucified before Christ.
I died in my murdered mother's womb
and came back to life to be beheaded.

I am a citizen of nowhere.

I think you will find
that I possess the best credentials
to qualify for martyrdom.

Lost

I've walked along the road of spiritual negation
so many times it's given me blisters.
There's no spring in my step anymore.

My Polish chiropodist cares for my tired feet
and makes me smile. She is a source of light
as she treats each toe as an errant individual
that deserves attention.

She has plasters and creams at her command
when she talks of pogroms
and sighs.

She knows about history. She's sceptical.
That's why she brightens me.

When the worst darkness descends,
I dial her number.

Levelling

My mother washed and scrubbed the underwear
of a duke and duchess
and a Scandinavian prince
and quite a few Honourables
and – oh, she couldn't count how many –
lords and ladies.

There were some upstarts, too,
the ones who put on airs,
the kind who thought their shit was scented soap
by all appearances.

She could put names to all the stains:
'That one's the Countess,' or
'That's bound to be the bishop,' or
'That one's young Alexander, if I'm not mistaken.'

'I've got a knowledge that you'll never have,
my clever son,' she boasted.

Of course she had. It fed her sarcasm.
Her eyes had seldom had the wool pulled over them.
I never asked her if the duke and duchess,
the prince, the Honourables, the lords and ladies,
the parvenus, the countess and the bishop
and the messy Alexander
had ever deigned
to thank her for her services.

Maternal (1984)

We sat, the two of us,
hand in surprised hand,
saying nothing.

Words were beyond us.
There was brightness enough in the room
as the afternoon darkened.

I thought, when I rose to leave,
that this was the happiest conversation
we'd ever had.

Corporeal

I lost my libido during radiotherapy.

I could concentrate at last, I told myself,
on higher things.

I felt no sense of deprivation.

I was no longer restless down below.

It was as if I was pre-pubertal –
an innocent, inquiring boy again,
looking uncloudedly
at the wide, vivid world before him.

But then, once the treatment was over,
the old Adam returned
slowly, determinedly,
with his promises of bliss

and I feel imprisoned once more,
inclined to the wild unreason
that's unbecoming in a man my age
and seeming dignity.

Transplant

If there's a single part of me
that's beneficial to a dying person,
they're welcome to have it.

I almost relish the idea
that the recipient of my one functioning organ
might be a serial killer
or a lying, deceitful, rabble-provoking
politician.

But then, on the other hand,
if I'm hoping against hope –
to use those comforting clichés –
that carefully, hygienically removed
part of the man I was
might be the cause of a love renewed
and welcomed and cherished
and gratefully acknowledged.

But I'll be ashes then.
I'll have no reason to apologise
or to celebrate.

Renown

Nobody praised you before you were born.

No one could see you coming.

You weren't afforded anyone's attention.

The vast unhonoured ranks of the dead
found different ways of passing the limited time
allotted to them.

They never bothered themselves
with what you'd be doing
when you had the chance
to show your singularity.

The letters 'f' and 'a' and 'm' and 'e'
spell 'hunger' in Italian.

And that's what you have now –
a hunger for more years, perhaps,
more weeks and months,
more vivid, living moments.

Aqueous

I love the mournful beauty of anemones.
They're heavy drinkers. You can almost sense them –
after a day or two trapped in a vase –
groaning for water.

Ranunculi are much the same.
They're brighter than their purple cousins –
flauntingly yellow, gayer in spirit –
but just as thirsty.

Why do these guzzling flowers call to mind past grief?
I had their need for water once,
though more dramatically.
I craved a final immersion.

It wasn't coming. The rivers I was drawn to –
the Thames, the Arno, and the Tiber –
all offered invitations I declined.
I stared at them beseechingly, and fled.

Poem

My last of days was there to contemplate
when words absconded from me
as long ago as nineteen-forty-one.
I must have heard the nurses talk of death.

My last of days was often in my mind
when I was decked out in school uniform,
clutching my mother's hand for the assurance
it wasn't in her nature to provide.

My last of days was an obsession with me
in all the years I was romantically inclined.
I cherished the idea of being doomed.
My happiest day was when a stranger said
I looked like Keats.

My last of days was cast aside
for glorious intervals
when I began to function in the world.

My last of days returned to me
with the last days of friends I loved.
I suffered an abundance of them.

My last of days is getting closer now.
I fear I have to welcome it.

The Lollipop Man

He lived in Florence, in a small, ground-floor apartment near Piazza Santa Maria Novella, within walking distance of the railway station. His specialist skills were most in demand during the football season, when the local team Fiorentina was playing at home. It was then that his clients came from Turin and Milan, or Rome and Naples, each armed with a bottle of cheap red wine in lieu of payment.

Vincenzo, my Florentine friend, took me to a nearby trattoria on that mildly sunny afternoon in October 1968, because he had a *molto shocking* surprise for me which we had to witness by sitting outside. He ordered Negronis for us and some delicate *biscotti* and we settled down.

A man appeared from one of the buildings on the opposite side of the street and placed a table, covered with an embroidered white cloth, on to the pavement.

– That's him, said Vincenzo. Watch carefully.

I watched as the man went back into his flat and reappeared with a large carafe of red wine and three glasses. He put these on the table and disappeared again, returning seconds later with a bottle of water and another much smaller bottle containing, as far as I could see, a pale green liquid.

– His mouthwash, Vincenzo informed me. Very important.

The man sat down, consulted his watch, and poured himself a generous glass of wine. He lit a cigarette.

– He's ready for business. The match finished ten minutes ago, so the fun should be starting very soon.

I had no idea what he was telling me.

– Be patient.

The man was middle-aged and bald. He was plump rather than

fat. He looked cherubic, I said, with his face set in the half-smile that cherubs have in certain paintings.

Vincenzo revealed that the cherub was called Signor Lecca Lecca. The Lollipop Man.

– Look, look, he said, with sudden excitement. They're arriving. There must be – yes, ten, no, fifteen of them. Oh, he's going to be busy today.

– *Buona sera, ragazzi*, said the beaming Signor Lecca Lecca. Some of the youths, all wearing identical shirts and scarves and pom-pom woollen hats emblazoned with the name of their team, responded to his greeting. The ones who didn't seemed embarrassed and nervous. They giggled and punched each other in a friendly manner before standing in line, as was the custom demanded by the obliging gentleman who would be doing his best to cater to their needs.

– He's advising them, in purest Tuscan, to show him respect.

I was beginning to understand what was happening, I said. What intrigued me was the indifference of the passers-by, who brushed past the waiting youths without a backwards glance. It was as if Vincenzo and I were the only spectators.

The ageing cherub took out his teeth, dropped them into a glass and covered them with water. He clicked his fingers and the first youth in the line followed him into the apartment.

– *Molto shocking?*

– *Moltissimo.*

After the tenth bottle had been left on the table and the cherub had come out of his lair at intervals to guzzle straight from the carafe or gargle with the green liquid, we decided it was time to eat. When the waiter came back with the food and wine we had ordered, he asked us if we were enjoying the street theatre. Vincenzo assured him that we were, although his English friend was a little shocked.

The line grew longer. The football fans – some of whom, Vincenzo informed me, were probably good Catholic boys and therefore virginal – seemed to be happy with the service the toothless lollipop man had provided. They had lost their nervousness and were singing and shouting while they waited for the friends who had yet to be seen to joined them to go home.

At six o'clock, there were twenty-eight bottles of red wine on Lecca Lecca's table.

– He deserves a place in the *Decameron*, Vincenzo said. It's an irony that Boccaccio, whose name can be translated as 'dirty mouth', never writes about blow-jobs. There might be a reference to cunnilingus that I missed when I studied it, but I can't remember one. What a life Lecca Lecca's had and what a wonderful story Boccaccio would have made of it.

It took the cherub, whose gleaming teeth were now back where they belonged, several minutes to carry the bottles, the glasses, the table and the chair into the apartment. He was very drunk. A young man, older than the youths, started talking to him. It was clear what he wanted, but Lecca Lecca was in no mood to comply. He began to shout that he was tired and that business was finished for the day.

– *Chiuso, chiuso, chiuso*, he screamed.

The man said something so nasty that Lecca Lecca spat at his retreating figure.

– He called our friend a sucker of cocks, which is a statement of fact when spoken politely, Vincenzo explained. But when it's said with contempt, it's horrible. Even lollipop men deserve a rest, don't you agree?

Devotion

Thirty years after his death
she visits his grave again.
after twenty-eight years.

She was anticipating decay –
the grass grown wild above and around it,
with dandelions perhaps
the only flower to honour him.

She sees, instead, that someone has cared for it.
The headstone gleams brightly.
There are sweet peas in the vase
his mother cherished.

There is his name. There are his dates.
And there's the sonorous epitaph
she chose for him back then
still visible.

Cookery

At six o'clock this evening
I picked up the phone and dialled a number
that's been in my head for more than a third of my life.

Somebody answered.
It wasn't her.
Of course, of course, of course
it wasn't.

I said I was sorry.
'No problem, my friend,' was his reply.

And then I heard her calling me
a silly goose.

And then I sat and thought of her
for desolate hours on end.

And then I reassured her
that as soon as autumn came
I'd make the curried parsnip soup
she'd invented.

Jordanian

In chapter five of the second book of Kings
Naaman, a 'mighty man of valour' who was also a leper,
dipped himself seven times into the River Jordan, where
    his leprous skin
'came again unto the flesh of a little child',
making him clean for ever.

The jordan I knew when I lived with my dirty granny
had nothing in common with the holy, cleansing river.
It was the name of the po in which she did her business.

My very clean mother always referred to chamber pots
and in the special hospital where my life was saved
the nurses persuaded me to sit on the potty
when I awoke in panic in the middle of the night.

But Granny's jordan wasn't for others' use.
Her jordan was *her* jordan, decorated as it was
with faded flowers that might have been violets once.
It was, she liked to claim, 'historical'.

The jordan, the chamber, the piss pot and the po
were emptied every morning by my uncle George –
the youngest of her thirteen children –
into the bucket in the garden shed
he called the shithouse.
He'd trailed a rose bush over and around it,
making its outside fragrant in the summer
while flies buzzed merrily inside.

Whenever I read the metaphysical poets
or the great, anguished divines
and see the word Jordan coming towards me
I have to blink away those might-have-been violets
and that foul gazebo.

Heavenwards

I've taken to wondering
if Traherne, before he saw
eternity the other night,
had gone to the lavatory
and emptied his bowels
of earthly matter.

Or, perhaps, it was after his vision
that he, replete with gloriousness,
suddenly found himself
like other mortals.

I see him on the hillside
and inside the privy
and marvel at his poem.

Lateness

after Friar Thomas of Hales, circa 1250

When my eyes mist over
and my ears start singing
a constant, tuneless music
and my nose snivels in the cold
and my tongue turns heavy as lead
and incapable of speech
and my complexion fades
and my lips lose their redness
and pucker
and my mouth is given to gaping
while spittle drips out of it
and my hair takes to standing on end
when I misplace my comb
and my heart is quaking
at the thought of the greenness
that has gone from me
and my veiny hands tremble
and my feet are stiff and solid
beneath me –

It is then that I know it's late.

Absence

I'm talking to a friend who's lost his mind.

He's somewhere else.

I am the only one who hears what I'm saying.

I settle for silence.

He's nodding agreement now.

The longer I'm silent, the more he's alert.

'You're so, so right,' he suddenly exclaims
to nothing I've said.

Finale

You were a cunning trickster to the last.
I heard your last breath.
I saw your last, faint, smile.

I went on watching you
in numb amazement
while every mark of winter
vanished from your face
until you were almost young again.

You looked improbably benign –
or so it seemed to me –
and glowing, for heaven's sake,
instead of glowering,
as was your custom.

You'd stored up this serenity –
somehow, somewhere,
out of common sight –
to celebrate our last reunion.

Askew Road

I remember that the resurrected man was wearing a floppy bow tie and a suit made of pale blue corduroy. His long blond hair was clean and well-brushed, falling neatly onto his shoulders. He had bright eyes and rosy cheeks. It was difficult to believe in his assertion that he was newly returned from the dead.

He was standing outside a funeral business berating the director of another funeral business on the opposite side of the busy street. There was a lavish funeral, of a kind rarely seen these days, in progress. A black-coated, top-hatted coachman was tending two plumed white horses in preparation for the ceremonious drive to the cemetery. The carriage bore a large coffin bedecked with white lilies which had been arranged by a resourceful florist to spell the word DAD at five different angles – on the top, and on both sides and at both ends. Four black Bentleys were lined up behind. The director and his staff wore top hats and tail coats and the mourning women's faces were partially hidden by black veils.

The resurrected man was not impressed.

'This is a ridiculous extravagance. If you must force me to repeat myself, I will do so. Please inform this Dad person's family that they are wasting their money.'

'How many times do I have to ask you to show some respect? These good people are grieving.'

'They'll be grieving even more when you send them the bill.'

'Watch what you're saying.'

'I speak from grim experience, I'll have you know. Do please listen carefully. The Other Side, the Great Beyond, or Heaven, or Paradise, or whatever other hyperbolic euphemism you choose to employ, is not worth the cost of the journey you are about to embark on. I have been there. You are looking at a man who escaped. Am I making myself clear to you? I've visited the "undiscovered country" and I died all over again from boredom.'

'Don't make me laugh,' said the director, smiling.

'I was hoping to become acquainted with a devil or two, but no such luck. I was spared the company of angels, though, for which I am – if you will allow me to use the expression – eternally grateful.'

'Good day to you, young man. It's been a pleasure talking to you.'

'I can't return the compliment. I wish I could, but I am unable to do so. You seem intent on ignoring my warning words of advice.'

'That *is* my intention, yes. Now go on your way and leave everyone in peace.'

A small crowd had gathered, and was still gathering, around the resurrected man. He looked radiant as he said, 'You are my witnesses. Cast your eyes on the farcical spectacle happening before you.'

But the witnesses were regarding him as the farcical spectacle. 'You're the best free entertainment in London, mate,' one of them remarked. 'You're a right bloody posh clown.'

Then they applauded him and, after a pause, so did the undertakers and the coachman and the mourners and even the skinny child who would be acting the role of mute in the forthcoming procession.

Bacchanal

Leave the wine on the table.

There's one stubborn leaf left on the cherry tree,
combating coldness.

Let's honour its disdain for winter
by raising our glasses.

Open that other bottle.

Let's see if it survives
what remains of the night,
our resilient companion
in longevity.

O. Henry

Cemetery

The plastic flowers are blooming today
and bees are feasting on their sudden pollen.

Stone cherubs and angels are dancing
the tango and the paso doble.

They're throwing parties in the mausoleums
and celebrating something.

Jesus and Allah and Buddha
are swapping dirty jokes.

The earth is heaving with laughter
and spring's in the air on this winter morning
and I'm happy to be with the riotous dead.

Drought

He loathes the weeping in Romantic verse,
the constant sorrowing.
Give him a break.
He knows when he's been thunderstruck by grief
he hasn't wept.
The absence of tears was telling him
he'd seen the worst.

1939

What I remember now
is the faint glow of the paraffin lamp
and the warmth of the darkness
in the unlit half of the room
where I felt at peace
with cocoa to drink.

Harmony

For J.

How resonant silence is
when it's only ours to share,
when it makes a peculiar music
that is seldom silent.